BEAST, TO BE YOUR FRIEND

✳

JENNIFER MOSS

BEAST, TO BE YOUR FRIEND

＊

JENNIFER MOSS

＊

NEW MICHIGAN PRESS
TUCSON, ARIZONA

NEW MICHIGAN PRESS

DEPT OF ENGLISH, P. O. BOX 210067

UNIVERSITY OF ARIZONA

TUCSON, AZ 85721-0067

<http://newmichiganpress.com/nmp>

Orders and queries to nmp@thediagram.com.

ISBN 978-1-934832-19-6. FIRST PRINTING.

Printed in the United States of America.

Design by Ander Monson.

Cover photograph by Elijah Gowin, courtesy of
Robert Mann Gallery.

CONTENTS

For my family—

FIELD

Nothing about her
let me think
she wasn't
a real
goat until I
saw the straw
hat behind
her hips she
said: "I see you're
a goat too."

THE PET

The door knobs shimmer.
Tears can trickle somewhere leaving their salt skins.
I am a lover of light,
my claws click in the cool halls.

The boy sleeps alone tonight in his long nursery;
in the night the pulse stops in his wrists and groin.
His lips are sour, he has left his mind
like a flower found on a walk and carried

but put back on the path.
I'm not afraid of domestics with their dull teeth,
there is sugar in the rice,
bicycles are ringing with pleasure,

over the bed purple drapes across blue.
Here's what I might choose:
robes and rubber balls, soldiers, upholstery,
I show the tall woman I'm not afraid

of loud talk in salons,
not of the marble green bust of my sister.
They are all naughty and free
to give nothing or everything,

they kiss my pink tongue.
Workers are loading the linens and opening vents,
they've pinned a white ribbon into my hair,
wiped up my chin, orders are growing below;

here comes sunlight on the silk sheets,
shit in the ruffles,
someone is shrieking his name, I know they have maps,
but they don't come back, they don't use them.

A MAN HAD A BIRD

that clutched my finger
and moved its voice
over bits of song.
It was this man's idea
to teach his bird
the funny tunes he knew.
Its throat,
in the puffed-up
down, was a thin
and knotty cord.
Its feathers were gray
and did not smell
of anything.
Its eyes were black
or dark brown
and their surface
held the room
in miniature. It seemed
to have a reason
for its singing
and stopping
that had less to do
with pleasure
than with exactitude
in sound.
It took the silly notes

the man gave out
and gave them back to him.
I think he liked
to hear his songs
arrange the bird's new memory.
I think he loved the bird
the way a small boy
loves himself
inside his doll.
He dangled shiny strings
of metal beads
and the bird
pulled violently at them.
He laughed
and shut them in a drawer,
then held a piece of
mirror up to the bird's
face: he said
this always worked
to make it sing again.

FIELDS

The calf across the drift of grass called us.
Through the fields we heard the wind
clatter on the metal sheds,
on the stiff, gray blades of windmills.
The fields were cold
and the sharp plants came up to our chins.
We sang, the dirt warmed,
we took off our jackets, rolled up our sleeves.
The cows across the fields
wound like a slow, chestnut ribbon.
Sentences uncoiled over the square acres turning silver,
our faces tilted into the odorless sun.
And the machines on the horizon looked like toy machines,
bright with sun.
And the cows across the fields in the feedlots
were bright with sun.
The distance pulled us forward.
The strict distance where we fastened down the land
in nervous sentences.
The sky was sharp and clear.
We moved between rows, male and female.
Sometimes the taste of herbicide.
Sometimes the scent of infection.
Sentences slipped into blithering.
The bloated cows looked like toy cows,
eating pharmaceuticals from the troughs.

We licked our hands where the cuts had opened.
Words slipped into heavy breathing.
Machines churned through the receptive stalks.
A Cessna flew over the hills.
Through the hybrids our heads moved against the blue
screen of sky and sounds of exhaust and lowing
turned through the air.

MAKING THE CENTAUR

It seemed the horse arrived with the wind,
and the white flash of his eyes suggested

thoughts that were three-fourths fear,
the tingle in his nerves racing toward injury.

In a sudden kick and burst through the fields
he was chased by earth's symbols,

all beauty turned hostile.
A spiral in the wild sky noosed him,

terror cinching him up hoof to head,
and the clouds appeared, after, always arranged by pain.

His will now tangled fiercely with yours,
it rains all day on the tin roof,

foam smeared over his flanks,
his mental heat phantoming.

All day his voice twisting in the air.
Then, toward night, there is the break:

the deep restraint you recognize in the rope,
some strength the horse keeps in darkness.

A new creature rises up between you.

DUCKING IN AND OUT OF SHADOWS

Ducking in and out of shadows, I thought:
the sun does always make me lengthen.

I thought it as a form of meditation.
As a labyrinthine message to something that watches.

I felt the watcher but was afraid to speak.
So I drew it closer with my fear.

And what I feared came.
Alone over the rocks.

A goat from a distance walking toward me.
I felt a debt to the goat

walking from that distance.
The broken branches

there in the wide clearing.
A silver thread blowing in and out of visibility.

The goat's womanish head bobbed up and down.
When she reached me, one yellow eye turned toward the sun

The goat was a body filled with disease.
I put a rope around her neck

and led her to a treeless field.
And hit her with a switch.

Her legs shattered when she sprang.
The goat lay in the dust,

her bloated belly heaving.
Under my shadow, lengthening.

Which became longer the deeper she breathed.
Which grew great and covered us both.

I shook and cried under the sky over the goat.
And this kept us alive.

THREE OCTOPI

Three octopi on a platter of ice.
Six aristocratic eyes.
Raise the cutlery and slice.

—How was your life?
—Green and wide.
—Will the sky die? Will it break like glass?
—We are just three octopi.

Three octopi on a platter of ice.
They are glistening, preposterous and smooth.
Through the windows the mountains are precise.

IN MAMMAL HALL

What keeps me staring
is the absence of this zebra,
looking so present.
When I watch without blinking,
it looks like he's breathing.
Getting closer I see the place
where they slit him open,
the narrow, stitched seam in the hide
running along the belly, up the legs,
breast, neck, to lower jaw.
I meet his glass eye with my eye.

Because he's empty, this zebra is mine.
I fill his body with my mind
to give my thought a shape.
In the painted desert scene behind him
other zebras graze and nap,
but he's not interested in them.
He's standing on his wooden mount
staring through the glass
as if some sharp urge had pierced his heart
and frozen him in space.
The border of the brain turns cold.

COW

In her expression
is some skepticism.

BEASTS FRAMED THE FIELD I

Beast there is sun on your red belly
You lick yourself clean
smooth your legs and chest
the ax of your heart chops
through the forest   no rest
You have grown around your teeth
and instantly your eyes tighten on a target
My dogs won't answer to their names
they run off in their thick coats
Why not love the Other
playing his violin
Beast you lived a hidden life
now go away to sniff and dig
let's see your talent for living

BEASTS FRAMED THE FIELD II
(A BEAST SPEAKS)

There your egg-shaped head
lit from behind
Your force sits in a room
I don't think you've felt your solitude
as much as you will at my paws before we
crash over the fossil bed
Your glasses stare at that dark window you keep touching
and talking to   Through the window
I can look you clean in the face
see the vein jump in your neck
and the salt shining over your lip
Could it be you want to rub your head against mine
Do you want our fur to crackle
Do you want to dig a hole in the field
dig back to your red and black birth
with me chasing after
Do you want each twist toward mother to hurt
and do you want to do it again

BEASTS FRAMED THE FIELD III

Because I am a trapdoor, hallucinating,
things seem, then things end.
Behind a door a red beast fought:
terse, acid, electrical with fear.
(In my eyes I saw the beast's eyes
filled with death, like fluorescent lights).
What would we do without the accusing sky above our heads?
I put the innards there to please the sun.
From the house, smoke rises like seraphim.

BEASTS FRAMED THE FIELD IV

Beast to be your friend I'd gather the clouds swarming
    over the river
I'd play the horn of forgiveness all night
I'd plant a garden in your name
and we could drink our milk together
To be your friend I would stop my voice
be still as a stump
so you might finally lie down beside my lap
and lick my hand and look into my eyes
You are a good Beast and to be your friend
I'd like to see your eyes soften
and I'd like to see your eyes follow my gaze
I'd like to see your eyes fill with worry when I set my sights
on another   and I'd like to see
your jealous eye look after me   a tremble down your spine
I'd like to see you at my leg when I walk
I'd like to feed you from my hand the suffering inborn
disease of my blood
I'd like to make your home between my walls
I'd like to hear you speak   tell me where I'm from
it's all gone underwater
I'd like to be your friend

BEASTS FRAMED THE FIELD V
(A BEAST SPEAKS)

Then the ambush from all sides.
The joys of the fight for the field!
Among the joys were a branching wind
and skies rushing over startled skins.
When my teeth caught your thigh
you rattled for the first time like an alien.
Thrust through the swift grass, your features distended.
Your voice, enchanted, came to life.
Your days of misfortune ended.

FROM SICKNESS

From sickness, what do you hear?

    The tick of a floorboard
    swelling in the heat.

How deep do you sleep in sickness?

    Words lose their cargo,
    their sounds float free,
    and we find them *interesting*.

        To the sparrows an ox sings
        I am a small ox
        walking in a dark field.

    In the funnel of ears
     In the doorway overheard
      In dizziness

What does sickness mean?

    To fear the Lord
     (God's full attention upon us)
    is sickness made meaningful.

        I will change.

We look out from sickness
and read the signs.
The signs sit in everything.
They are true, but untranslatable.

What will be my end?
 What is moving me?
  Shall I walk through the field?

And the question over and over to myself:
 who am I?

and the answer:
 I am two: I and you

ARTHUR GANSON'S *MACHINE WITH WISHBONE*

The wishbone walks like a drunk man, or a baby,
each step teetering barely into the next.
Its legs are clasped with metal cuffs.
From the cuffs, two slender rods run back to
the machine—an elegant invention of five wire wheels,
the largest two, like toy carnival rides, turning above.
Delicate gears, sprockets, spokes and springs
whir with a ghostly precision.
The wishbone, its neck stunted, without a head,
has a bottomless innocence, so earnest and submissive
it makes us want to look away.
Far behind, the machine pushes it slowly,
like a silver dream guiding the bone's destiny.

PORTRAIT

What withdrew from us   What moved
away over the buildings where there was
an inch of sun in the heavy sky
then looking over we thought we knew
nothing of it   The ambulance turning
its quiet lights   radio static through
the wide-angle view
of a parking garage   At the top two policemen
standing near a man sitting
at the edge   their stillness long
On the street the crowd abuzz   and a chant
jump   jump   laughter   someone said
he'd been up there two hours
still no action

*

What I thought by the darkening wall
three crows calling out suddenly
to work the air with complicity   such musical
blank time   The linear ornamental flowers
in a box   I felt the life-span
and a fumbling   Ideas they
don't matter   Who knows
how to look at the person next to you
he is tight breath and blue beneath
the skin   The chains on the flagpoles squeak out
forgiveness   fast blink

*

There is a skywalk
people meet there in the rain
and sun asking for innocence
leave off go looking for the doorway
I saw one segment of cloud
turn green and spread   A man looking down
from above   a crowd looking up

*

What breath on the forehead
What anima   the crickets drown
Take away the buried thread
Take away the father knife
What river   take away the shine

*

You know he is going to die
sometime   everything does   The reddening
trees beat out sound with their elastic
branches and sugar   still the world depends on
him   wind dissolves in his veins
nothing exists by itself but now
he is alone   The man next to me watches him
through binoculars "*This* is drama"
He says it to his friend   Does he see
his life in the life of the man up above   He
is taut with anticipation   he opens his
great throat   the world is fresh and young

*

The buildings are momentary and reveal themselves
bold magnificence eked out into
this radiant strain of weather   A camera
passes through the street   its shadow
of conscience for a moment unbearable
Then composed things appear

THE STORM

Where one mind stops,
another begins.

Where cutlery shines on plates,
a voice lowers.

One length of forgiveness,
round and round like a child's game
in the dust.

Outside, the rain formalizing.

When we leave we are replaced.

Shaky clouds in lightning,
my shadow alive on the floor.

Then the small passage for sleep.

How green and spidery the sky.

In its net, the dead bees of memory.

ACKNOWLEDGMENTS

Thanks to the editors of the following magazines, where many of these poems first appeared:

Another Chicago Magazine: "Portrait"
Caliban: "The Pet"
Conduit: "Beasts Framed the Field III," "Beasts Framed the Field IV"
Denver Quarterly: "Beasts Framed the Field I"
Hayden's Ferry Review: "A Man had a Bird"
The Literary Review: "From Sickness"
River Styx: "Three Octopi"
3rd bed: "Ducking in and out of Shadows," "The Storm"
West Branch: "In Mammal Hall," "Fields"

✳

COLOPHON

Text is set in a digital version of Jenson, designed by Robert Slimbach in 1996, and based on the work of punchcutter, printer, and publisher Nicolas Jenson.

JENNIFER MOSS was born in Spokane, Washington. She received a BA from Grinnell College and an MFA from the Iowa Writers' Workshop. She currently lives in Seattle. Her poems have appeared in *Pleiades, Indiana Review, Denver Quarterly, Image,* and *Conduit,* among other journals, and she has received grants from the Washington State Artist Trust, as well as a Literary Artist Award from the Seattle Arts Commission.

✸

NEW MICHIGAN PRESS, based in Tucson, Arizona, prints poetry and prose chapbooks, especially work that transcends traditional genre. Together with DIAGRAM, NMP sponsors a yearly chapbook competition.

DIAGRAM, a journal of text, art, and schematic, is published bimonthly at <http://thediagram.com>. Periodic print anthologies are available from the New Michigan Press.

www.ingramcontent.com/pod-product-compliance
Lightning Source LLC
Chambersburg PA
CBHW020953030426
42339CB00004B/75